LATERAL
THINKING

50 BRAIN-TRAINING
PUZZLES TO CHANGE THE WAY YOU THINK

LATERAL
THINKING

CHARLES PHILLIPS

CONNECTIONS
BOOK PUBLISHING

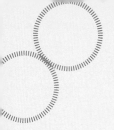

For Alison, Melanie, Jim, &Tom

A CONNECTIONS EDITION
This edition published in Great Britain in 2011 by
Connections Book Publishing Limited
St Chad's House, 148 King's Cross Road, London WC1X 9DH
www.connections-publishing.com

British Library Cataloguing-in-Publication data available on request.

ISBN 978-1-85906-283-8

1 3 5 7 9 10 8 6 4 2

Phototypeset in Bliss using QuarkXPress on Apple Macintosh
Printed in China

CONTENTS

How to Think Laterally

We don't always see what is right in front of us. We may see what we want to see or are predisposed to see. We may be convinced that what we are seeing is all that there is to see. But perhaps—unawares—we're looking from the wrong angle or even in the wrong direction.

There is almost always more than one way of looking at a problem. It can be easy to overlook the most productive or creative way of tackling things. When we're faced with a problem that seems insoluble, we often need a fresh emphasis or approach to find the way forward.

Lateral thinking is a set of strategies for changing the way we look at the world, for finding unexpected solutions, for thinking in new directions. One of the keys to the approach is understanding perception—how and why we see things in a particular way, why we miss things, and how to shift perspective. How to see things laterally—or sideways.

THROW OUT THE RULES The idea of lateral thinking was developed in 1967 by the British psychologist and author Edward de Bono. He likens thinking to a game of chess. You play chess with set pieces—the knight, queen, bishop, and so on—and according to agreed rules. Similarly, we usually think in assumed concepts and along familiar lines, the equivalent of the chess pieces and principles.

We should be ready, he says, to disregard these concepts and rules in order to find new ones—to play the game with different pieces and regulations. We might ask ourselves, are these rules the only options? We might say, are we asking the right questions? We might consider, is this problem really a problem?

This approach isn't necessarily hard work. Effort is no guarantee of success in thinking laterally. In fact, when we try too hard, we may become trapped in rigid patterns of thought. What we need instead is skill and applied intelligence.

We need to relax. A light-hearted approach is more likely to help us succeed. We should look closely, follow our interests. Research on the brain shows that we often think best when we're engaged with a problem and enjoying ourselves.

WHAT DOES THIS LOOK LIKE? In learning to think laterally, a reliable strategy is to reposition yourself mentally. Question assumptions. Faced with a lateral-thinking problem, consider key questions like these:

- What does this look like?
- Could it be viewed from another angle?
- If it's a verbal puzzle, are there words that could be misleading—what else might they mean?
- If the problem consists of a described scenario, is it really a complicated description of something very simple?

Another aspect of this fruitful approach is to ask "What if?" questions. Throw away your preconceptions. Say, "I'm taking that for granted, but if I don't then what would I see or think?" Ask yourself, "What happens if I combine those two elements? Can I get away with skipping that stage? Can I approach this from a completely different angle?"

GET READY TO CHANGE Did you know that your brain contains one hundred billion brain cells called neurons and that each one can make connections with thousands or tens of thousands of others? That each second your brain makes a million new connections? We all have an enormous capacity to change and to learn, and none of us should ever feel trapped in one mental approach. If you consider yourself a logical person, who likes to think in straight lines, you can train yourself to think laterally, starting with the carefully designed puzzles we have set out for you.

THE PUZZLES IN THIS BOOK There are three levels of puzzles, each with a "time to beat" deadline. These deadlines apply a little pressure—we often think better when we have goals such as time constraints. But don't worry—if you find you take longer than the "ideal" time, relax. Take as long as you want if faced with a particularly perplexing problem—the important thing is to try to think in the way outlined. Some puzzles also have a similar version later in the book to give you even more practice.

Look out for puzzles marked Time Plus. You'll almost certainly need a bit longer to complete these—not because they are more difficult as problems but because there's more work to do before you can solve them. Where we feel you might need some help, a tip has been provided, and there are Notes and Scribbles pages later on for note-making and scribbling! Also toward the end of the book, the Challenge is designed to give your newly acquired lateral-thinking skills a good solid work-out. This has a suggested time limit of 10–15 minutes to give you a chance to consider and reconsider the challenge, think around and away from the problem, perhaps make a few notes.

You'll find that as you develop your lateral-thinking brain you will quickly feel the effect at work or college and in other areas of your life—by seeing things clearly, and being creative and quick to adapt. The benefits are many. So, start thinking laterally, and turn the page!

PUZZLE GRADING	TIME TO BEAT
EASY = WARM-UP	1–2 MINUTES
MEDIUM = WORK-OUT	3–4 MINUTES
DIFFICULT = WORK HARDER	5–6 MINUTES
TIME-PLUS PUZZLES	6+ MINUTES
THE CHALLENGE	10–15 MINUTES

50

puzzles for

LATERAL
THINKING

Remember
Throw out the **rules**!
Don't think **too** hard
Take your **time** and **free your mind**
to think **LATERALLY**

EASY
puzzles for
LATERAL
THINKING

The puzzles in this first section of the book give your
lateral-thinking skills a warm-up. They're designed to
provide practice in seeking out new perspectives. Try to
look at problems with fresh eyes. Take a step back and
question what you're seeing or reading.
Surprise yourself—sometimes we need a little shake-
up to shift ourselves from established, routine
patterns of perception and thought.

LINE THEM UP

Two old friends, Murphy and Vishal, can't help spotting a puzzle everywhere they go. One fine day, Vishal challenged Murphy to alter the arrangement of six glasses, three full and three empty, lined up on the bar before them as shown.

"Touching just one glass, can you arrange these six so that they alternate one full, one empty, and so on?" asked Vishal. Can you help Murphy retain his reputation as Vishal's puzzling equal?

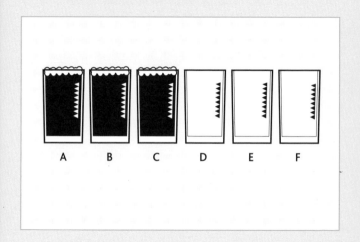

Think laterally—rather than literally—about how to solve the problem. Instead of starting with what you've got, try imagining what you want to achieve and work backward.

ONE INTO THREE

Find a fresh perspective. Can you see your way to dividing this abstract form into three identical shapes, using just two straight lines?

To solve this problem you need to be able to see not just how to split the shape into three but also how to "flip" the three segments so that they are identical.

13

PUZZLE 3 WARM-UP

A CLEVER SQUARE

Four matches are arranged to make a Greek cross (that is, one with four equal arms). Can you make a square by moving just one of the matches?

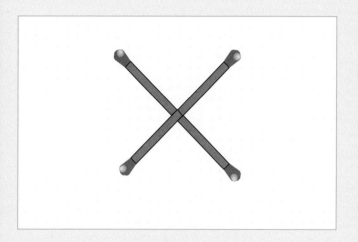

Squares come in many sizes.

FOUR-STAR

Here's another test for your ability to visualize connections between disparate items and plot an overall pattern. Which four shapes—two black and two white—can be fitted together to form the star shown at the left? The pieces may be rotated, but not flipped over.

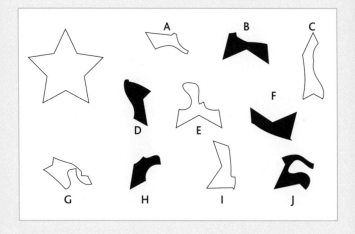

Look out for outlines that match neatly.

HOME PARKING

The Hamilton children have passed their driving tests with flying colors, but their success has created a potential space problem at home. When each car the family owns occupies one of the parking spaces outside the house, one has nowhere to go. But these are modern fuel-conscious vehicles. They are so tiny that—with skill—you can park two in one parking space.

Today the whole family parked their cars outside the house and there is still one whole space left unoccupied. How can that be? How many cars do the Hamiltons own? And how many parking spaces are there outside their house?

To fit their vehicles in, the family takes a doubly lateral approach to parking.

ARE YOU SWITCHED ON?

Moving into your new house, you discover three light switches downstairs. One of them turns the light on in the garage, the other two do nothing. You can't see the light coming on from where you are, so how can you find out which is the right switch, and only have to make one trip to the garage?

A   B   C

how to think TIP

The mental energy you generate considering this little problem should really warm up your powers of lateral thinking. Think about it ...

FOUR BY FOUR BY FOUR

This cube originally measured four blocks high, deep, and wide. Assuming that all the blocks that can't be seen from this angle are present, how many blocks have been removed?

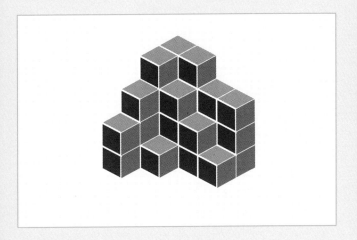

how to think TIP

To work this out, you need a strong spatial sense and good powers of visualization to imagine and then hold in your head an image of the complete cube before counting the missing blocks. Lateral-thinking tests often require an ability to hold visualized images in your mind, and turn them about while you consider different angles.

TIME TRAVELER

James is making a business trip from London to Mumbai (Bombay) in India. For the duration of his trip, he deliberately wears his wrist-watch upside-down. Why?

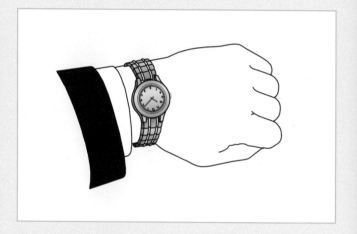

 James hates digital watches and always wears an analog watch. Have you tried telling the time on an analog watch turned upside-down?

TRIANGLE 2 SQUARE

Raj is a bright mathematics student who likes his job selling newspapers because he loves meeting people. Sometimes when things are slow he rearranges the change on his counter. Here he has laid out nine coins in a triangle. How many will he need to move in order to change the triangle to a square?

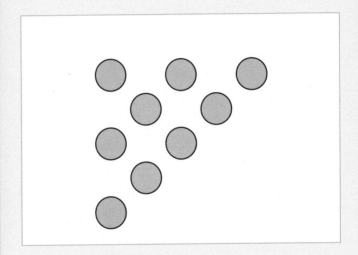

This kind of exercise in visual logic makes a great warm-up for lateral thinkers. You need the ability to play around with objects in your mind's eye and try out creative combinations when you're doing lateral-thinking tests.

AS SEEN FROM ABOVE

You'll need to use your imagination to work out what these simple drawings represent. Things are not always what they appear to be at first sight, as we find again and again in lateral-thinking exercises.

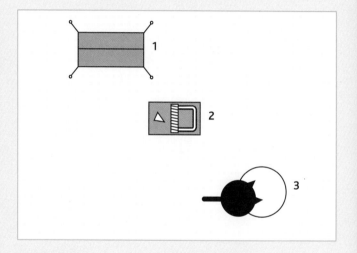

how to think TIP

Imagine you have a bird's-eye view.

NUMBERED AMONG THE GREATS

Millie's got some amazing news for her soccer-mad dad, Tony. She's going to meet one of the all-time great players when he pays a visit to her college. Tony loves puzzles, too, so Millie sends him this drawing with the message: "Decode the soccer legends to work out the name of the player I'm going to meet."

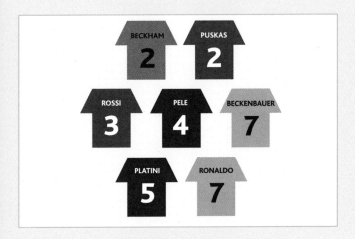

Lateral thinkers practice code-breaking because lateral problems often need to be read, reread, and interpreted. The meaning of the problem is often deliberately obscured by misleading language.

22

IMPOSSIBLE TRIANGLE?

Sasha's job selling maps gave her an idea for a way to puzzle her friends. She asked them: "How can you draw a triangle on a piece of paper so that all three interior angles are right angles (that is, 90 degrees)?"

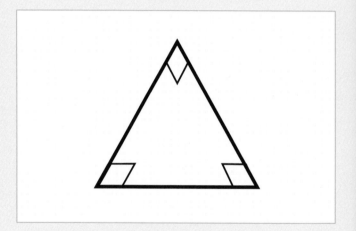

The lateral challenge lies in thinking where Sasha might put the piece of paper. Think about where she works.

GEOMETRIC WORLD

It's all about perception. In a parallel universe you might be able to perceive things only in terms of geometric shapes. Can you make a lateral shift to re-imagine these drawings as real objects?

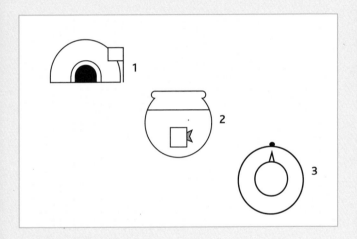

 how to think TIP

Brrrr! You'd be feeling chilly if you were near 1 or 3.

MISSING LETTER

Which letter of the alphabet can you add to continue this straight-forward series?

A, B, C, D, –

how to **think** TIP

Beware: The answer is not E.

PUZZLE 15 WARM-UP

BUSHY-TAILED HORSE

All but one of these pieces can be fitted together to form the rearing horse shown here. Which one is not required? You can rotate the pieces, but not flip them over.

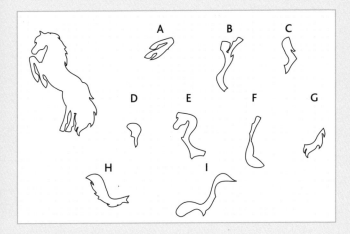

If you find this one's tricky, you could copy the outlines onto paper and play about with them.

ART AND MONEY

Samantha has convinced Art Mobley, the owner of the Manhattan art gallery at which she works, to try out a new pricing policy. Can you decode the policy and work out what this recently acquired painting by Toulouse-Lautrec should cost?

Picasso $16,000,000

Van Gogh $22,000,000

Matisse $13,000,000

Toulouse-Lautrec ?

how to think TIP

In Samantha's lateral policy for the art market, no artist is worth more than $26,000,000.

MEDIUM
puzzles for
LATERAL
THINKING

We're moving on to medium-difficulty puzzles to give your developing powers of lateral thinking a more demanding work-out. By now you probably have a clearer idea of the kind of sideways shifts that are often required in tests of lateral thinking. Remember to think again, or take a second look—you often need to question the one aspect of the image (or piece of information) that you're most likely to take for granted.

FIVE BY FIVE BY FIVE

Our work-out starts off with another chance to practice thinking in three dimensions by completing a cube with missing blocks. Did you develop a useful strategy to help you solve Puzzle 7? This time the cube originally measured five blocks high, deep, and wide—how many blocks have been removed? You should assume that all the blocks that cannot be seen from this angle are present.

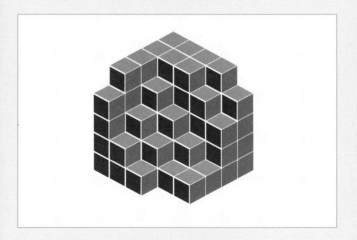

 how to think TIP

You could try calculating the missing blocks on each level of the cube, then adding these numbers up. You'll need to be good at holding the image in your mind.

SCOTT'S LATERAL DICE GAME

Schoolboy Scott has come up with this way of playing dice silently with his friends Walter and Wilson so that their teacher won't notice. Sitting in a row—supposedly reading from their textbooks—they take it in turns to jumble the dice over in one hand then slide them along the table. To make it more interesting the score is the total of the spots not visible. Scott has just had his go. What's his score?

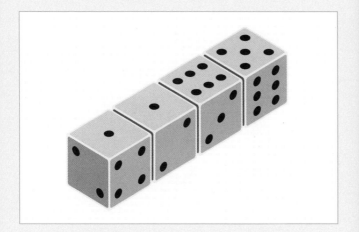

It will help to start by working out the total of spots on a single die. While you're at it can you think of any other lateral ways for Scott to play dice silently so his teacher doesn't hear? There's no right or wrong answer—just a chance for some more lateral practice. Compare answers with friends or family members.

A REWARDING HOLIDAY

Aunt Lucia lives in Miami. Last summer she took a two-week cruise around the islands and countries of South America. Two days after she returned home, she took another cruise on the same ship, staying in the very same cabin. The second time was just a two-day trip along the coast of Florida. She enjoyed both trips, but she came back from the second one $50,000 richer. How?

how to **think** TIP

After reading this paragraph, consider for a moment exactly where Lucia went on each trip.

PEARL'S CHALLENGE

Cashing up at the end of the day in her store, Pearl set a challenge for her manager, Courtenay. She laid out money in the arrangement below and asked: "Can you move just one bank note so that both the horizontal and vertical lines add up to the same amount?"

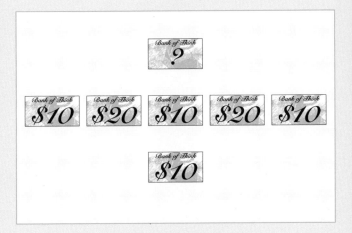

 Courtenay is scratching his head looking at the notes on the counter, but he needs to reconsider the question and think exactly what it might mean, as should you.

FOURSOME

Four of the shapes below (two black and two white) can be fitted together to form the regular heptagon (seven-sided shape) on the left. Once again you have to work in two dimensions—you can rotate the pieces, but not flip them over.

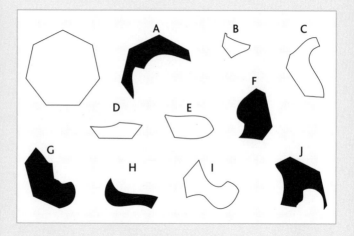

Look for pieces that can be rotated to align with the outer edge of the heptagon.

THE HIGHWAY CODE

When this sign appears beside the road in Saul's video game, he realizes that the game's asking him to break the code that produced such crazy distances.

Can you help him break the highway code and work out how far it is to Chicago in his game?

LOS ANGELES 240
LAS VEGAS 120
NEW YORK 70
CHICAGO ?

how to think TIP

Tell Saul to try letter-counting.

A BELT THAT WEARS ITSELF

The industrial conveyor belt shown below suffers wear and tear on the outside but is untouched on the underside. What simple modification can you make, without needing extra machinery, so that the conveyor wears evenly on both sides?

how to think TIP

Is it possible to turn a two-sided strip into a one-sided strip?

YANG'S DILEMMA

A rich Chinese businessman is none too pleased that his daughter Yiyun wants to marry a humble musician, Yang, and hatches a plan to ensure that it doesn't happen. He tells the couple that a happy marriage must be blessed with good fortune, and before he gives his own blessing to the wedding, he wants to see if luck is with them. He organizes a meal for both families, at the end of which a golden plate containing two fortune cookies arrives at the table.

"One cookie says, 'Your marriage is blessed,'" the father explains. "The other says, 'You must part.' The fortune you choose will tell me whether your union has the approval of the stars." He holds the plate under Yang's nose. Yang suspects (rightly) that the father is trying to trick him, and that both fortune cookies are going to say "You must part." What can Yang do to keep his bride without causing a family scandal?

LOOK AGAIN

You will need more than one look to determine what these drawings represent. The twist in these lateral images often resides in the artist's choice of an unexpected vantage point or the reduction of real-life objects to the most basic geometric forms.

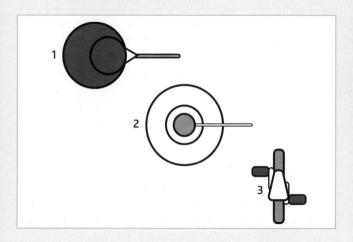

how to think TIP

Think where you might be looking from as well as what you're looking at.

DIGITAL DANCE

For the Mathematicians' Convention, Dr. Mocherla comes up with a neat sequence of numbers to dance along the wall-mounted digital display. He offers his latest book as a prize to the first delegate who can work out the code and predict the next number.

Alvin wins the prize. What number does he predict?

3, 8, 15, 22,

32, 42, 51, 58,

70, 79, 88, ___

how to think TIP

Think laterally—look beyond the sequence of numbers. What other characteristics do they have?

KAVITHA'S RINGTONE

Kavitha is given a new mobile on which she can program the ringtone of her choice. She creates the code shown on the musical stave below to make a tune from the name of her favorite Western classical composer. Can you crack her code to work out whose music she likes best?

how to think TIP

Kavitha seems to like repeating notes. Forget what you know about the letter values of musical notes—think laterally.

BUTTERFLY JIGSAW

All but one of the pieces can be fitted together to form the butterfly shown in the top-left corner of the box below. Which one is not needed? As before (see Puzzle 4), the pieces may be rotated but not flipped over. Exercises like this, as we have seen before in the book, hone our re-evaluation skills. We learn to combine close observation with shifts of perspective, and these are key strategies in lateral thinking.

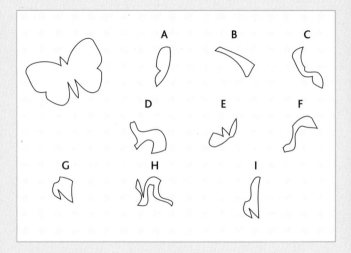

Look for edges and outlines that may fit neatly together.

106 UP

This is a test of our ability to see numerical combinations and plot possible changes. In the square below, leave 42 of the 49 numbers exactly where they are. Change the positions (but not the values) of the remaining seven, in such a way that in each horizontal row, vertical column, and long diagonal line of seven squares, the seven numbers total exactly 106.

18	22	8	12	22	26	6
8	20	9	15	24	19	13
7	10	16	25	11	20	14
12	6	25	8	18	15	21
24	11	20	18	7	17	16
10	26	17	6	16	11	8
15	19	13	21	7	5	25

how to think TIP

For this puzzle you have to get adding. Doing mental math quickly is a very effective way to stimulate your brain and build connections between brain cells. This puzzle also hones your visual logic skills.

SHAPE SHIFTER

Exercises like the Shape Shifter challenge below and the number grid opposite hone our ability to see connections clearly and interpret what we see. For the Shape Shifter challenge, can you determine, in terms of units, the total length of the perimeter of this shape?

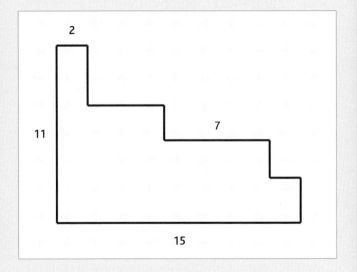

The clue is in the title. Look beyond the shape's current form.

TAIWO'S MAP

Taiwo is an amateur coin collector. One day when she goes out with her metal detector, she finds several coins but doesn't have time to dig them all up. So she makes a grid map showing their locations. After a misunderstanding, Taiwo is given a three-hour detention at school, but she passes the map to her twin Kehinde and asks her to dig up the money while it's still light. Can you help Kehinde make sense of it?

In a note, Taiwo tells Kehinde about her ingenious system. Taiwo writes: "Where a number appears on this grid, it shows how many coins are located in the squares (up to a maximum of eight) surrounding the numbered square, touching it at any corner or side. The squares with numbers written in them do not contain coins. There is only one coin in any individual square." Can you help Kehinde by placing a mark in every square containing a coin?

	1					3	
0	1	2			2	3	
			4	3			
1							1
		1				4	
	2		1			4	
		1	1			4	
2	2				0	2	
			0			3	
		1					
3			2	1			
1					1	0	

SIX BY SIX BY SIX

This puzzle takes our lateral visualization test (see Puzzles 7 & 17) to the next level. Try again to judge how many blocks have been removed from the large cube. Its original dimensions were six blocks high by six deep and six wide. All blocks that cannot be seen from this angle are present.

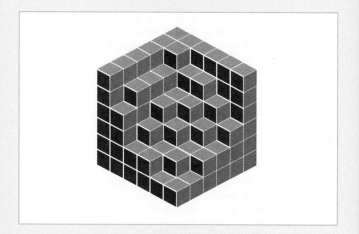

Work up from the bottom.

45

LATERAL PICTURES

The latest brain science suggests that our brains work by means of a rolling process of making predictions based on evidence combined with past experience. We then re-evaluate the predictions in the light of what we discover in examining things in more detail. We may give too much weight to past experience. These lateral drawings require us to step sideways from our first response to consider what the images might also represent.

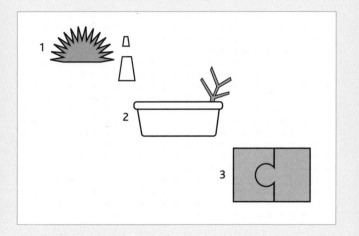

Two of these contain creatures.

THREE IN ONE

Can you cut two straight lines through this shape to create three identical segments? In the light of brain scientists' theory about the brain's reliance of prediction (opposite), it's interesting to consider whether it's harder or easier to do an exercise like this when the object in question doesn't look like anything concrete. Is it a distraction when you think "Oh that's a pair of legs," say, or does it help you?

As with earlier puzzles of this kind, try turning the book around in your hands to see the shape from different angles—or try visualizing it from a lateral (sideways) perspective or from behind.

DIFFICULT
puzzles for
LATERAL
THINKING

You'll have to work harder at the puzzles in this third
part of the book, which contains the most demanding
of our exercises in lateral thinking. A good strategy is
to use analogies, to ask yourself "What is this like—and
why it is like that?" Sometimes it helps to try to
"inhabit" a problem, to imagine yourself within it.
Always aim to find a fresh perspective and to
adopt a canny approach.

HIDDEN NUMBERS

What number should take the place of the question mark next to the fourth die?

 Consider the title to this puzzle.

SMART SQUARE

Can you use two straight cuts of equal length then rearrange the pieces to form a perfect square?

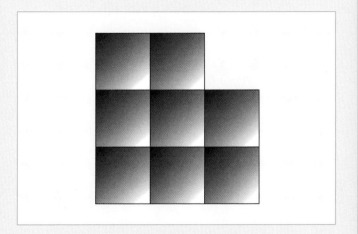

Look for ways to make up the square's outer perimeter.

WHERE ARE YOU?

The three clocks indicate the name of a capital city. Can you crack
the code to work out where you have landed?

They may be 24-hour clocks!

UNEXPECTED PERSPECTIVE

You may need to shift your perspective in working out what these drawings represent.

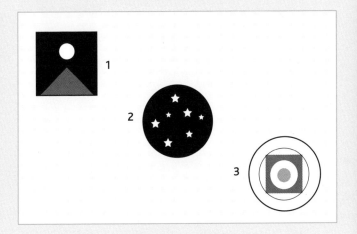

What time is it? Think where you might be looking from as well as what you're looking at.

KAKURO

Stretch your mathematical abilities to the limit with this laterally shifted number grid, in which you have to work backward to determine constituent numbers from totals. The clues to the puzzle appear within the grid: Each blank square should contain a single digit number from 1–9; every set of numbers across or down has a sum total equal to that of its clue, shown either directly above or directly to the left. See the example (above right).

	21	13	
17	9	8	6
11	7	3	1
12	5	2	5

THE FORDS' ANNIVERSARY DINNER

In the ship's restaurant one Friday night, Mr. and Mrs. Ford ordered a lobster supper. Partway through the feast, they called over Tony the head waiter for a word, and he in turn sought out the manager, Rocco, who glided over to the table. "Congratulations," said Rocco, "I understand today is your wedding anniversary?"

Mrs. Ford beamed. "That's right," she said. "We were just wondering if the restaurant would like to help us celebrate with, say, a bottle of champagne?"

"Of course, Madam, it would be our pleasure. How long have you been married?"

"28 years today," Mrs. Ford gushed. "It was a truly beautiful ceremony. We married on a Sunday and the church was strewn with fresh rose petals. We drove off to our honeymoon—a cruise, of course—in a vintage Bentley."

The manager smiled blandly and walked over to the head waiter.

"They're trying it on," he whispered to Tony. "Give them a cheap bottle of cava, and if they grumble, sling them out."

Mr. and Mrs. Ford were indeed trying it on, but how did Rocco know?

THREE-WAY SPLIT

Professor Greenacre brings his love of geometry into the kitchen with him. His homemade pie has come out of the oven in a very precise geometric form. How should the professor cut the pie, in two places only, so that he has three identical portions to share with his friends, Dr. Gupta and Mr. Gosztony?

Try a number of perspectives to see the effects of rotating parts of the design.

A STRIKING CLUE

Chief Inspector Cope found this matchbook in the abandoned hotel room of international diamond smuggler Juliana Maggiore. From it he was able to work out her destination. Where was Juliana headed?

Switzerland
Turkey
Iceland
Lebanon
Greece
Ireland
Norway
Sweden

how to think TIP

Is there more than one relevant meaning for the word "capital?"

COFFEE-TABLE CHALLENGE

Max places four dice on a coffee table. Jordan, sitting directly opposite, can see the top four faces of the dice, as well as a further five faces Max cannot see. Neither Max nor Jordan can see the bottom faces of the four dice. What is the total number of spots on all the faces of the dice that Jordan can see, given that this is different from the total number of dots that Max can see?

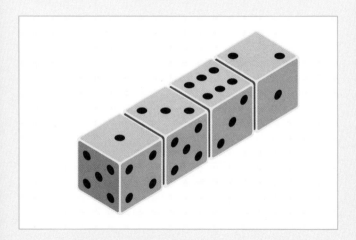

 how to think TIP

It might help if you were to think "around" the question.

TEATIME FOR ALICE

Professor Greenacre's up to his geometric cooking tricks again (see Puzzle 41). He has baked a perfectly square cake, then cut it in three different ways, so that each time the amount of cake on either side of the cut is equal. He offers his granddaughter Alice a piece. She knows she wants piece A or piece D, but can't decide which is larger. With no extra information, can you see a way to help Alice work it out?

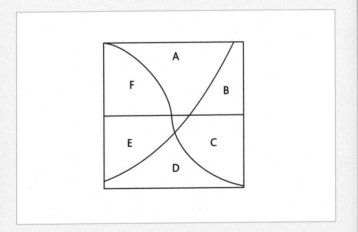

A little knowledge of simple equations is the key.

KETTLE POSER

All but one of these pieces A–J can be fitted together to form the kettle shown at the top left, below. Which one is not required? Remember, as in our earlier puzzles of this kind, you may rotate the pieces, but not flip them over. Can you see the connections? Look— and look again.

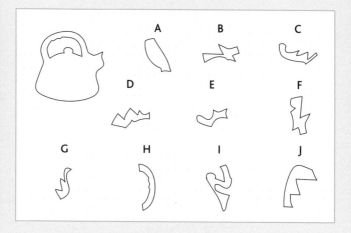

Identifying the kettle's handle among the pieces gets you off to an easy start.

FIERCE FACES AT THE FAIR

Professor Finnegan took her three smart children, Eve, David, and Samson, to a fair, where they all got their faces painted. But with no mirrors around, none of the children knew which design they had received. Professor Finnegan saw this as an opportunity to test the children's lateral-thinking skills.

"You are all either a tiger or a lion," she told them. "Put your hand up if you can see a tiger!" Three hands went up. "Good! Now put your hand down when you know what you are."

There was a pause. Then Eve slowly lowered her hand. "I'm a tiger too!" she said.

But how did she know?

KEHINDE'S MAP

Kehinde has borrowed an idea from her twin sister Taiwo (see Puzzle 31). She took Taiwo's metal detector and went to the beach to get rich. She found several coins in the sand but didn't have time to dig them up all before dark, so made a lateral thinker's grid map showing their locations just as Taiwo did.

As before, where a number appears on the grid it shows how many coins are located in the squares (up to a maximum of eight) surrounding the numbered square, touching it at any corner or side. The squares with numbers written in them do not contain coins, and there is only one coin in any individual square. Kehinde has to go to collect her mother from the airport, so she gives the map to her friend, Reggie, and asks him to find the coins and dig them up. Can you help Reggie by placing a mark in every square containing a coin?

			1			2	
4	4				2		
		3					3
3					1		
1			1		3		
		2				2	2
	2	2	1				
		1			3		2
4					3		
					2	1	
4		3	1				2
					1		

130 UP

As in 106 Up (Puzzle 29) the test here is to plot numerical combinations so that rows, columns, and diagonals make matching totals. In the square below, leave 42 of the 49 numbers exactly where they are: Change the positions (but not the values) of the remaining seven in such a way that in each horizontal row, vertical column, and long diagonal line of seven squares, the seven numbers total exactly 130.

37	24	26	18	15	33	8
29	18	14	34	6	6	22
15	18	8	2	22	30	16
7	2	34	28	18	13	34
21	30	17	31	35	5	4
17	13	33	7	3	23	28
35	6	4	23	7	19	12

The only way to solve this puzzle is to start adding!

PUZZLE 49 WORK HARDER

WHAT ARE YOU DOING?

Imagine what you might be doing to see the views below. These puzzles represent a good exercise in lateral thinking because they require you to come at the question from a quirky angle.

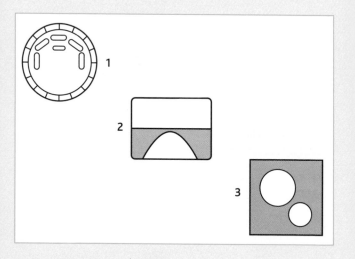

 Try imagining yourself standing in the scene.

SQUARING UP

Which six shapes—three black and three white—can be fitted together to form the perfect square in the left-hand corner of the box? You may rotate the pieces, but you are not allowed to flip them over.

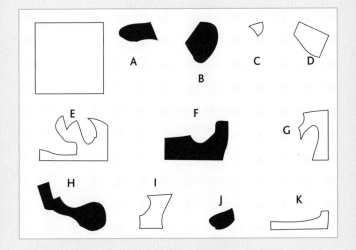

Look out for angles and outlines that match.

THE
CHALLENGE

This final section of the book gives you the chance to put some of the thinking skills you have learned so far into practice by working your way through a lateral problem set in the everyday world of job interviews and home-buying. If we understand thinking to be like a board game, as lateral pioneer Edward de Bono suggests, we now come to the stage of re-examining the rules, looking closely at the pieces, and even rethinking the game itself. We might want to question our aims and motives—just what are we trying to do? Where are we headed? What is this game for, and about?

DID YOU GET THE JOB?

The scenario that follows may sound implausible, and indeed it is, but it sets up a thorough-going test of your lateral-thinking ability. In the scenario you suffer a series of setbacks that threaten to ruin what you'd hoped would be a triumphant day—and the challenge is to work out what to do to resolve this difficult situation. Over the following three pages, then, be ready to look beyond the obvious. Read through the text three or four times, making notes in the side columns of clues or hints that you notice; think carefully about the situation described and what hidden elements or motives there might be. Question your assumptions. Be on the lookout for double meanings. Try to think through the full range of possible solutions and don't be afraid to head off in unfamiliar directions. You may need to approach problems from an unexpected angle, and to make creative combinations. Perhaps you'll want to question the very basis of the situation described.

Developing these capacities will stand you in good stead when you're next called upon to think laterally at work, when studying alone, or performing creatively in a group. You'll approach the problems with fresh thinking, a well-developed sense of your powers of perception, and a spring in your mental step. Now take a deep breath, clear your mind, and read on ...

You have a busy Monday morning. First of all, you have a job interview for a demanding and highly paid position. This goes very well. The interviewer seems positive and asks you several questions about yourself and what you are doing for the rest of the day. You give her all the details because you feel really upbeat—perhaps she's planning to call this afternoon to offer you the position.

Two hours later, you go to a prearranged viewing of an apartment in a new riverside block. It's marketed as a penthouse suite, with a superb river view. If you get the job, you'll make a down-payment. But when you arrive there, you find that the block is not quite finished.

You are handed a hardhat. A real-estate agent with a large bushy beard but a high voice takes you up in a lift to the top floor. Here, all is luxurious. The agent opens the door, and ushers you in. You gasp as you wander into the main lounge area and look at the extraordinary river view.

NOTES AND CLUES

69

NOTES AND CLUES

But then the door slams behind you, and you find you are alone in the apartment. You rush back and bang repeatedly on the door, but it does not open. Then you hear the agent walking calmly away, speaking on the phone. It takes a few moments of deep breathing before you calm down.

At last, you explore the apartment. It is bare. You look in the kitchen, bathroom, and bedrooms. All the fixtures and fittings are in, but there is no furniture.

You walk into the main lounge again. The floor is carpeted in white. In front of you are large French windows giving onto an expansive balcony. Beyond—far, far below—is the river, with a café alongside it that has many orange umbrellas.

On one wall is a large framed mirror with the letters ALICE written on it in red lipstick. It is too high on the wall to reach when standing. Nearby, in a small alcove, is what looks like a homemade apple pie.

In the center of the carpet is a coiled rope ladder. You consider your chance of climbing down from the balcony to the floor below—that shouldn't be too difficult. But when you try to open the French windows, you find they are locked with no visible keyhole. Instead they are fitted with a high-tech panel marked "Technicolor Word Security" and instructions to say a pre-set code word to open the lock.

Then you notice that on the balcony outside there is a mobile phone. It starts to ring ...

What do you do, or rather—how do you think?

NOTES AND CLUES

71

THE
ANSWERS

If you're really stuck, by all means enter this section, and find the answer to the problem that's stumped you. Try not to groan—it is a common characteristic of lateral-thinking puzzles for the solutions to seem extremely obvious when you see them! After reading the solution try to rehearse the stages of lateral thinking that led to the answer given, so that you pick up the strategy for future use. A number of our puzzles have another similar version later in the book to give you a chance to practice the relevant lateral skills. As with all puzzles, but especially lateral puzzles, it's possible that you may sometimes find an alternative solution. If so, well done! You are a true lateral thinker!

PUZZLE 1 LINE THEM UP After much deliberation, Murphy carefully empties glass B into glass E. This gives him the desired arrangement: full, empty, full, empty, full, empty. Simple puzzles like this are great for teaching your brain to tackle challenges laterally—in this case working from the result to finding the best possible method to achieve it.

PUZZLE 2 ONE INTO THREE This is good practice in shifting perspective. Brain science tells us that we think best when we're using many parts of the brain—here, developing your visual intelligence gives a boost to all your other ways of thinking.

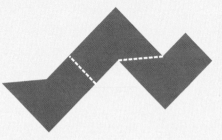

PUZZLE 3 A CLEVER SQUARE Move the match at the bottom-left slightly outward. A very small square is then formed in the middle of the diagram. This gives you practice in another key lateral-thinking strategy—interrogating the question. Read the question once, then again. Sometimes it's really asking you something slightly different from the one you see at first sight.

PUZZLE 4 FOUR-STAR

See the completed star (right)—
consisting of pieces I, B, G,
and H. This puzzle provides
good practice in visualizing,
comparing, and
manipulating patterns.

PUZZLE 5 HOME PARKING The Hamiltons own four cars, and
there are three spaces. Parking their tiny vehicles two cars to a space,
leaves one space completely free. My reference in the tip to a
"doubly lateral approach" hints at their solution, which is to park
sideways in twos.

PUZZLE 6 ARE YOU SWITCHED ON? Turn on switch A and
leave it for two minutes, then turn it off and turn on switch B. Go
quickly to the garage. If the lightbulb in there is off, but warm, it's
switch A. If it's on, it's switch B—and if it's off and cold, it's switch C.
It's easy to get trapped working out sequences of possibilities in
problems like these, but equally easy to take a simple sideways
(lateral) step such as considering "What is the side effect of turning
on a lightbulb?" The answer ("it gets warmer") leads you straight to
the solution. There was a subtle hint in the tip!

PUZZLE 7 FOUR BY FOUR BY FOUR There are 34 blocks missing from the original cube. There are 30 blocks in the picture and 64 (4 x 4 x 4) in the complete cube.

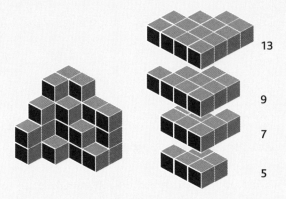

13

9

7

5

PUZZLE 8 TIME TRAVELER Mumbai is 5.5 hours ahead of London. Turning the watch upside-down allows James to convert between London and Mumbai time without resetting the watch, with only the hour hand slightly out of place.

PUZZLE 9 TRIANGLE 2 SQUARE
Two. Raj finds that these kind of light-hearted exercises really improve his ability to find solutions quickly to practical and mental problems.

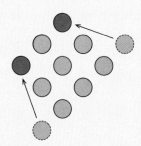

PUZZLE 10 AS SEEN FROM ABOVE
1 A tent (from above)
2 A mousetrap
3 A kitten drinking milk

PUZZLE 11 NUMBERED AMONG THE GREATS Here the title gives you a clue—the number on each shirt tells you which letter of each great name to take—the 2nd of BECKHAM; the 2nd of PUSKAS; the 3rd of ROSSI; the 4th of PELE; the 7th of BECKENBAUER; the 5th of PLATINI; and the 7th of RONALDO. Taken in order, these letters spell EUSEBIO.

PUZZLE 12 IMPOSSIBLE TRIANGLE? Sasha's store sold globes among the folding maps. She placed the paper over the globe, and drew from the North Pole down to the equator, along a quarter of the equator, then back up to the North Pole. A triangle of this sort is described as being "trirectangular" and can be drawn on the surface of any sphere.

PUZZLE 13 GEOMETRIC WORLD
1 Igloo for sale
2 A shy goldfish
3 A snowman (from above)

PUZZLE 14 MISSING LETTER The answer is the letter F, which can be placed on top of the underscore to form an E. The wording of the question leads us to think of the letters as a sequence, but the lateral shift comes when we consider the shapes of the letters and see that some letters have other letters within them.

A, B, C, D, E

PUZZLE 15 BUSHY-TAILED HORSE

D is not needed, as shown. The benefits for lateral thinking from an exercise like this lie in getting used to reviewing groups of shapes and trying out new combinations.

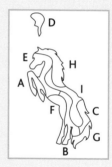

PUZZLE 16 ART AND MONEY Samantha's idea is to take the alphabetical position of the first letter of the artist's name and multiply it by a million. T is the 20th letter of the alphabet, so a Toulouse-Lautrec should cost $20,000,000.

PUZZLE 17 FIVE BY FIVE BY FIVE There are 45 blocks missing from the original cube, as shown below. There are 80 in the picture and 125 (5 x 5 x 5) in the complete block; another way of looking at it is that there are 25 cubes in each level of the block.

PUZZLE 18 SCOTT'S LATERAL DICE GAME There are twenty-one dots on each die, thus a total of eighty-four dots on the four dice. Since thirty dots are visible, the total number of dots on the sides that are not visible amounts to fifty-four.

PUZZLE 19 A REWARDING HOLIDAY Aunt Lucia is an art smuggler. She picked up loot in South America and hid it in her cabin. On the second trip she retrieved the hidden loot to take it home. Because the second trip was restricted to the United States, she didn't have to pass through US Customs on her way back.

PUZZLE 20 PEARL'S CHALLENGE Pearl was testing Courtenay's ability to interrogate the question. Are there any other meanings for the phrase "move one bank note" aside from the most obvious one? Instead of attempting to move the notes around, the way to make the horizontal and vertical lines add up to the same amount is for Courtenay to take a $50 note from his wallet and put it in the blank space.

PUZZLE 21 FOURSOME Pieces A, C, E, and H – see the completed heptagon (right).

PUZZLE 22 THE HIGHWAY CODE It's 84 miles to Chicago. The code works by multiplying the number of vowels in a city name by the number of consonants, then multiplying again by the total number of letters in the name: LOS ANGELES—4 vowels x 6 consonants x 10 letters = 240. The tip suggests letter-counting, but you need to make a lateral jump to consider not just the number of letters but also their type and the ways they combine. CHICAGO: 3 vowels x 4 consonants x 7 letters = 84.

PUZZLE 23 A BELT THAT WEARS ITSELF You need to put a half-twist into the belt, turning it into a Möbius strip. Now the belt has only one surface, which will wear out evenly. The Möbius strip is named after 19th-century German mathematician and astronomer August Ferdinand Möbius, a pioneer of topology (the study of what happens to geometric figures when they are bent or stretched). A Möbius strip is any continuous loop with a half-twist in it. You can make your own by taking a strip of paper, twisting one end by 180° and joining the ends. Your piece of paper originally had two sides, but now has only one.

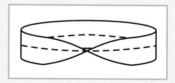

PUZZLE 24 YANG'S DILEMMA Yang eats the fortune cookie, message and all. Then the only way to find out what the message was is to open the other cookie. Since the other cookie says, "You must part," the one he chose first must have said, "Your marriage is blessed." He foils his future father-in-law without having to expose him for the scoundrel that he is.

PUZZLE 25 LOOK AGAIN

1 The early bird
2 A Martini
3 A unicycle

PUZZLE 26 DIGITAL DANCE The answer Alvin gives is 102. He understands that to obtain the next number in the sequence, you have to add the previous number to the number of segments that make up its shape. Since 88 contains 14 segments, the next number is 88 + 14 = 102. The title and the image help you make a lateral shift—the question only works with numbers produced in a digital display.

> 3, 8, 15, 22,
> 32, 42, 51, 58,
> 70, 79, 88, 102

PUZZLE 27 KAVITHA'S RINGTONE Kavitha's favorite composer is Jacques Offenbach. Her code works like this: Starting at the top of the stave, a single note on the top line is A, one on the second line is B, then C on the third line, and so on to E on the fifth line. A double note on the top line is F, followed by G, H, I, and J. A triple note on the top line is K, and so on.

PUZZLE 28 BUTTERFLY JIGSAW
Pieces A, B, C, D, E, F, H, & I combine to make the butterfly. Only G is unused.

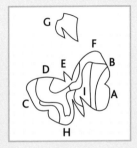

PUZZLE 29 106 UP

The seven numbers that need to be shifted are shown circled and in their new positions in the grid, right.

18	14	8	12	22	26	6
8	20	7	15	24	19	13
7	10	16	25	11	20	17
12	6	25	9	18	15	21
24	11	20	18	7	10	16
22	26	17	6	16	11	8
15	19	13	21	8	5	25

PUZZLE 30 SHAPE SHIFTER Fifty-two units. You just have to slide the sections along, as shown below, to make a rectangle. All the vertical sections make a complete 11-unit side, and all the horizontal sections comprise a 15-unit side.

The calculation of the perimeter is then quite simple: 11 + 11 + 15 + 15 = 52 units. The exercise requires us to look beyond the shape in front of us and consider what the shape means in terms of perimeter length.

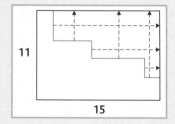

11

15

PUZZLE 31 TAIWO'S MAP The locations of the coins are shown on the grid. As Taiwo's instructions indicated, a square with a number 2 in it does not itself contain a coin but touches (at any corner or side) two squares that contain coins.

PUZZLE 32 SIX BY SIX BY SIX There are 70 blocks missing from the original cube, as shown below. There are 216 (6 x 6 x 6) blocks in the complete cube, and 146 in the partially complete cube. Taking the levels one by one, the missing blocks, as shown, number 3 on the first level, 10 on the second, 14 on the third, 19 on the fourth, and 24 on the fifth.

24

19

14

10

3

PUZZLE 33 LATERAL PICTURES

1 A hedgehog crossing the road
2 A reindeer taking a bath
3 The world's easiest jigsaw

PUZZLE 34 THREE IN ONE Two lines drawn as shown make three identical shapes from one. This kind of exercise is a very good example of how the solutions to lateral problems can be difficult to access but look extremely obvious when you work them out or are shown the answer. We can

all train ourselves to be better at particular kinds of looking and thinking. I used to find this kind of puzzle frustrating, but I have improved with practice over the years.

PUZZLE 35 HIDDEN NUMBERS The number is 9. The title suggests that you consider the hidden numbers on each die—the ones that are not visible. You can work out what they are because you know there are 21 dots on each die (1 + 2 + 3 + 4 + 5 + 6 = 21). But it's not as simple as merely adding up the numbers you can't see. By playing around with the available information with dice 1, 2, and 3 you need to make the lateral shift of seeing that to get the number you want, you add the numbers on the invisible faces of each die, separately add the numbers on the visible faces, then deduct the lower total from the higher total. There are 15 dots invisible on the fourth die and 6 dots visible, so 15 – 6 = 9.

PUZZLE 36 SMART SQUARE

The trick is to cut along the lines as shown, near right. This gives four right angles, which can be used to form the four corners of the new square, far right.

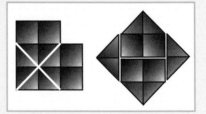

PUZZLE 37 WHERE ARE YOU? Berlin. The first clock is showing the time 02:05, the second 18:12 (6:12 in the evening) and the third 09:14. The letters of the alphabet in positions 2, 5, 18, 12, 9, and 14 are B, E, R, L, I, and N.

PUZZLE 38 UNEXPECTED PERSPECTIVE

1 A pyramid at night
2 Night view from a well
3 An egg on toast

PUZZLE 39 KAKURO

The answers are shown in the grid, right. For best results, do math problems like this as quickly as you can and don't be put off by the fact that the best method may be trial and error. Brain-training expert Dr. Ryuta Kawashima shows with brain imaging results that doing simple calculations quickly is (along with reading aloud) the best way to stimulate your brain. All kinds of thinking improve when you make your brain work hard.

1	3	2		9	2	1		6	9
3	9	8	2	7	6	5		9	7
	6	9	4	8	1		7	1	3
3	8		1	4		3	1	8	
9	7	8	5		8	2	5	3	1
		7	6	8	9	4		5	2
3	7		3	4	7	1	5	2	
6	9	8		1	5		8	4	2
	1	9	7	3	6	8		7	3
9	5		6	2	3	4	1		
7	8	3	9	5		5	2	3	1
	4	5	8		8	9		2	6
7	2	1		8	6	7	9	5	
8	3		3	5	9	6	8	4	7
9	6		1	2	4		5	1	2

PUZZLE 40 THE FORDS' ANNIVERSARY DINNER Rocco

knew that the calendar repeats itself every 28 years. If the Fords were married on a Sunday and today really were their anniversary, it would also be a Sunday—but, as we know, it's a Friday night.

PUZZLE 41 THREE-WAY SPLIT

Professor Greenacre makes the cuts in the places shown here.

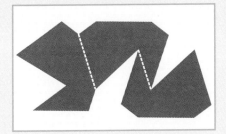

PUZZLE 42 A STRIKING CLUE Barbados. After several months on Juliana's trail, the chief inspector is able to break her code after a few minutes' work. Reading the list of countries on the matchbook, he works out that their capital cities are: Berne, Ankara, Reykjavik, Beirut, Athens, Dublin, Oslo, and Stockholm, and that the initial letters of the capitals combined spell Juliana's destination.

PUZZLE 43 COFFEE-TABLE CHALLENGE Thirty-one spots. Jordan can see the top faces of all four dice–a total of twelve spots. The opposite sides of a die have spots that add up to seven: So where Max can see four, five, three, and one spot, Jordan can see three, two, four, and six spots. On the bottom face of the farthest right die there are five spots, so the end face of this die (invisible to Max) has either three or four spots. If this end face has three spots, then the total number of spots Jordan can see is thirty. But the question says that Jordan can see a different number of spots from Max—and Max can see thirty. Therefore the end face that Jordan can see must have four spots. Thus Jordan can see a total of twelve spots on the top faces, fifteen spots on the side faces, and four on the end face, making a combined total of thirty-one spots.

PUZZLE 44 TEATIME FOR ALICE We know that each time the professor made a cut, the amount of cake on either side of the cut was equal—therefore D + E + F is half a cake, and so is E + F + A + (middle piece). Removing E + F from both sums, we find that D = A + (middle piece). Therefore, D must be larger. Luckily, Alice had just been studying equations at school and so eventually worked it out for herself—and this made the professor very proud.

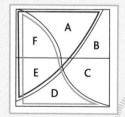

PUZZLE 45 KETTLE POSER

Only Piece B is unused. Just as in Butterfly Jigsaw (Puzzle 28) the intricacy of the object's outline makes this quite a challenge for your powers of visual imagination.

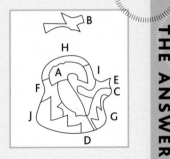

PUZZLE 46 FIERCE FACES AT THE FAIR

Eve can see that both her brothers have their hands raised and both are tigers. Eve knows that if she were a lion, David would see that. She also knows that David can see that Samson has his hand up (meaning he can see a tiger). She realizes that David (who is a super-smart kid, after all) could quickly work out that (i) if Eve is a lion and (ii) if Samson has his hand up because he is looking at a tiger, then (iii) David himself must be a tiger—and, having worked this out, David would put his hand down. But David hasn't put his hand down. Therefore Eve reasons (correctly) that she cannot be a lion, and so must be a tiger too.

PUZZLE 47 KEHINDE'S MAP

The locations of the coins are shown on the grid, right. The lateral thinker's grid map gives us good practice in thinking clearly and interpreting the code created by Taiwo and put to use by Kehinde.

●	●		1		●	2	
4	4		●		2	●	
●	●	3	●				3
3					1	●	●
1	●		1			3	●
		2	●			2	2
	2	2	1			●	
●	●	1			3	●	2
4				●	3		
●	●			●	2	1	●
4	●	3	1				2
	●				1	●	

PUZZLE 48 130 UP The seven numbers that need to be shifted are shown circled and in their new positions in the grid, right.

6	24	26	18	15	33	8
29	18	14	34	6	7	22
15	37	8	2	22	30	16
7	2	28	28	18	13	34
21	30	17	18	35	5	4
17	13	33	7	3	23	34
35	6	4	23	31	19	12

PUZZLE 49 WHAT ARE YOU DOING?

1 Stonehenge
2 The view from seat 148A (over the wing)
3 An easy putt

PUZZLE 50 SQUARING UP The three black pieces are A, F, & J; the three white pieces are C, E, & G. B, D, H, I, & K are not needed.

THE CHALLENGE: DID YOU GET THE JOB?

Once you are in the locked apartment, the object naturally seems to be to escape. The rope ladder provided on the carpet seems to confirm this suspicion—the obvious thing might be to try to open the window, then use the ladder to climb down. However, escaping is not the aim of the exercise.

What clues are there as to what is going on? ALICE is written on the mirror. To a lateral thinker this might suggest *Through the Looking-Glass, and What Alice Found There*, Lewis Carroll's 1871 children's classic; the thinker might consider looking through or perhaps behind the mirror. However, the mirror is mounted high on the wall. Now you might see a use for the rolled-up ladder—you could use it as a makeshift step to help you reach the mirror.

The next stage would be to take the mirror down and look behind—through the looking glass. Hidden there is a 4-digit pre-programmed safe.

This brings about a "Eureka!" moment. The discovery of the safe gives meaning to the apple pie you saw on the side – the pie suggests the code for the safe, the first four digits of π, 3.141.

So now you can open the safe, and inside you discover a key. If you try it on the main door, it will not work, but you keep looking. This stage of the solution emphasizes the importance of being patient with yourself when you are solving problems. You feel that you have found a solution but then you run into another obstruction. A lateral thinker stays calm, and looks for further clues.

Key suggests quay. If you look down at the quay beside the river, you'll see a café with many orange umbrellas. So, inspired by this, you try "orange" as the spoken security code for the door. It works! When you go outside the phone starts ringing again. You answer the phone: It is the job offer. The job interviewer explains she is looking up at you from the café far below. She explains that the test was not to escape, but to work out how to answer the phone after being locked in the apartment. She says that the real-estate agent with the high voice and the bushy beard was she herself in false-beard disguise. She congratulates you on your powers of observation, of deduction, and of lateral thinking and welcomes you into the company. Then she passes you on to the building's developers, who would like to talk to you about your plans to place a deposit on the penthouse flat.

Alice's Adventures in Wonderland and *Through the Looking-Glass* by Lewis Carroll, Penguin Classics 2003

The Art of Looking Sideways by Alan Fletcher, Phaidon 2001

Brain Book by Charles Phillips, Metro Books 2008

Cunning Lateral Thinking Puzzles by Paul Sloane and Des MacHale, Sterling 2007

Do You Think What You Think You Think? by Julian Baggini and Jeremy Stangroom, Granta Books 2006

Edward de Bono's website: http://www.edwdebono.com/debono/lateral.htm

H+ (Plus) A New Religion? By Edward de Bono, Vermilion 2006

Lateral Thinking: A Textbook of Creativity by Edward de Bono, Penguin Books 1990

The Leader's Guide to Lateral Thinking Skills: Unlocking the Creativity and Innovation in You and Your Team by Paul Sloane, Kogan Page 2006

The Mind Workout Book by Robert Allen, Collins & Brown 2003

The Phantom Tollbooth by Norton Juster, Harper Collins 2008

Six Thinking Hats by Edward de Bono, Penguin Books 2000

Teach Yourself: Training Your Brain by Terry Horne and Simon Wootton, Hodder Headline 2007

Test Your Creative Thinking: Enhance Your Lateral Thinking – Learn to Think Outside the Box, by Lloyd King, Kogan Page 2003

The Thinker's Toolkit: 14 Powerful Techniques for Problem Solving by Morgan Jones, Three Rivers Press 1998

Train Your Brain, by Ryuta Kawashima, Penguin 2007

The Upanishads translated by Eknath Easwaran, Nilgiri Press 2007

Upgrade Your Brain: Boost Your Memory, Think More Clearly and Discover Your Inner Einstein by John Middleton, Perigee Books 2007

The Use of Lateral Thinking by Edward De Bono, Penguin Books 1990

NOTES AND SCRIBBLES

the how to think series

Puzzles to help you ...

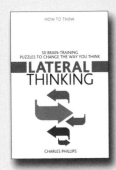

**... think
LATERALLY**
to solve
problems

**... think
CREATIVELY**
to generate
fresh ideas

**... think
LOGICALLY**
to make
reasoned
decisions

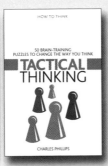

**... think
QUICKLY**
to cope in a
crisis

**... think
TACTICALLY**
to work out
strategies

**... think
VISUALLY**
to improve
communication

The Author

Charles Phillips is the author of 20 books and a contributor to more than 25 others, including *The Reader's Digest Compendium of Puzzles & Brain Teasers* (2001). Charles has investigated Indian theories of intelligence and consciousness in *Ancient Civilizations* (2005), probed the brain's dreaming mechanism in *My Dream Journal* (2003), and examined how we perceive and respond to color in his *Color for Life* (2004). He is also a keen collector of games and puzzles.

EDDISON SADD EDITIONS
CONCEPT Nick Eddison
EDITORIAL DIRECTOR Ian Jackson
ART DIRECTOR Elaine Partington
DESIGNER Malcolm Smythe
PRODUCTION Sarah Rooney

BIBELOT LTD
EDITOR Ali Moore
PUZZLE-CHECKER Sarah Barlow

PUZZLE PROVIDERS
David Bodycombe, Moran Campbell da Vinci, Puzzle Press

COVER DESIGN
Weiss/Werkstatt/München, Germany